CRAFTS FOR ALL SEASONS

CREATING WITH PAPER

Important Note to Children, Parents, and Teachers
Recommended for children ages 9 and up.
Some projects in this book require cutting, painting, gluing, and the use of small materials. Young children should be supervised by an adult. Due to differing conditions, individual levels of skill, and varying tools, the publisher cannot be responsible for any injuries, losses, or other damages that may result from use of the information in this book.

Published by Blackbirch Press, Inc.
260 Amity Road
Woodbridge, CT 06525

First Edition

Originally published as: *Juega con papel* by Roser Piñol

e-mail: staff@blackbirch.com
Web site: www.blackbirch.com

Printed in Spain

10 9 8 7 6 5 4 3 2 1

Library of Congress Cataloging-in-Publication Data
Piñol, Roser.
[Juega con papel. English]
Creating with paper / by Roser Piñol.
p. cm. — (Crafts for all seasons)
Includes bibliographical references and index.
Summary: Provides instructions for a variety of craft projects made mainly from construction paper.
ISBN 1-56711-434-2
1. Paper work—Juvenile literature. [1. Paper work. 2. Handicraft.]
I. Title II. Series: Crafts for all seasons (Woodbridge, Conn.)
TT870.P53513 2000 98-38941
745.54—dc21 CIP
AC

Contents

CRAFTS FOR ALL SEASONS

CREATING WITH PAPER

BLACKBIRCH PRESS, INC.
WOODBRIDGE, CONNECTICUT

A Wiggly Worm

1. Fold a strip of construction paper like an accordion. Take a piece of string and tie a knot at one end.

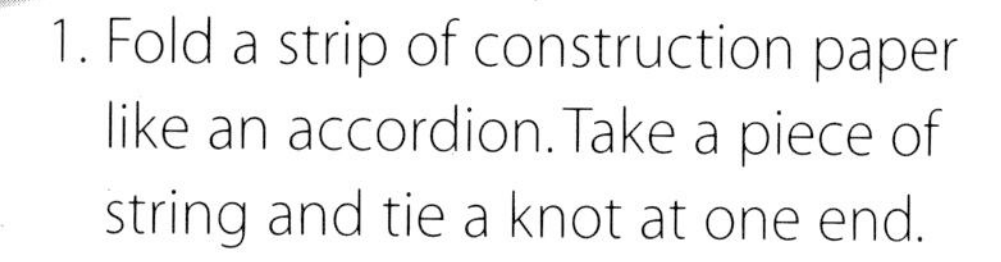

2. Cut the ends of the strip as you see in the photograph.

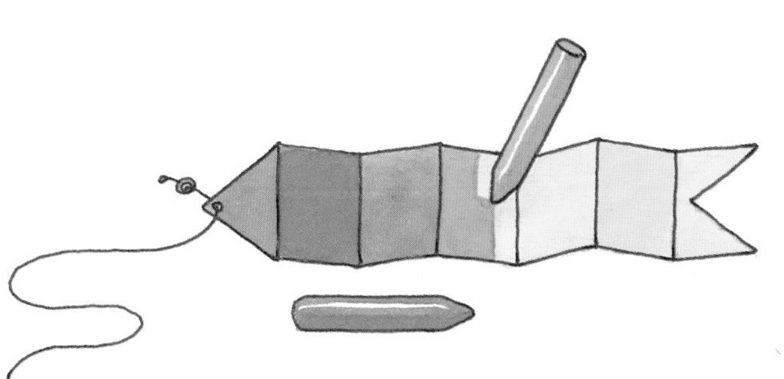

3. Color each fold a different color.

4. Cut a hole in the pointed end of the strip and run the string through it.

☛ ***YOU'LL NEED: a long piece of construction paper, a piece of yarn or string, colored markers, pencils or crayons, and scissors.***

5. You can make worms in different colors and sizes. You can make a pretty mobile or have a fun pull toy.

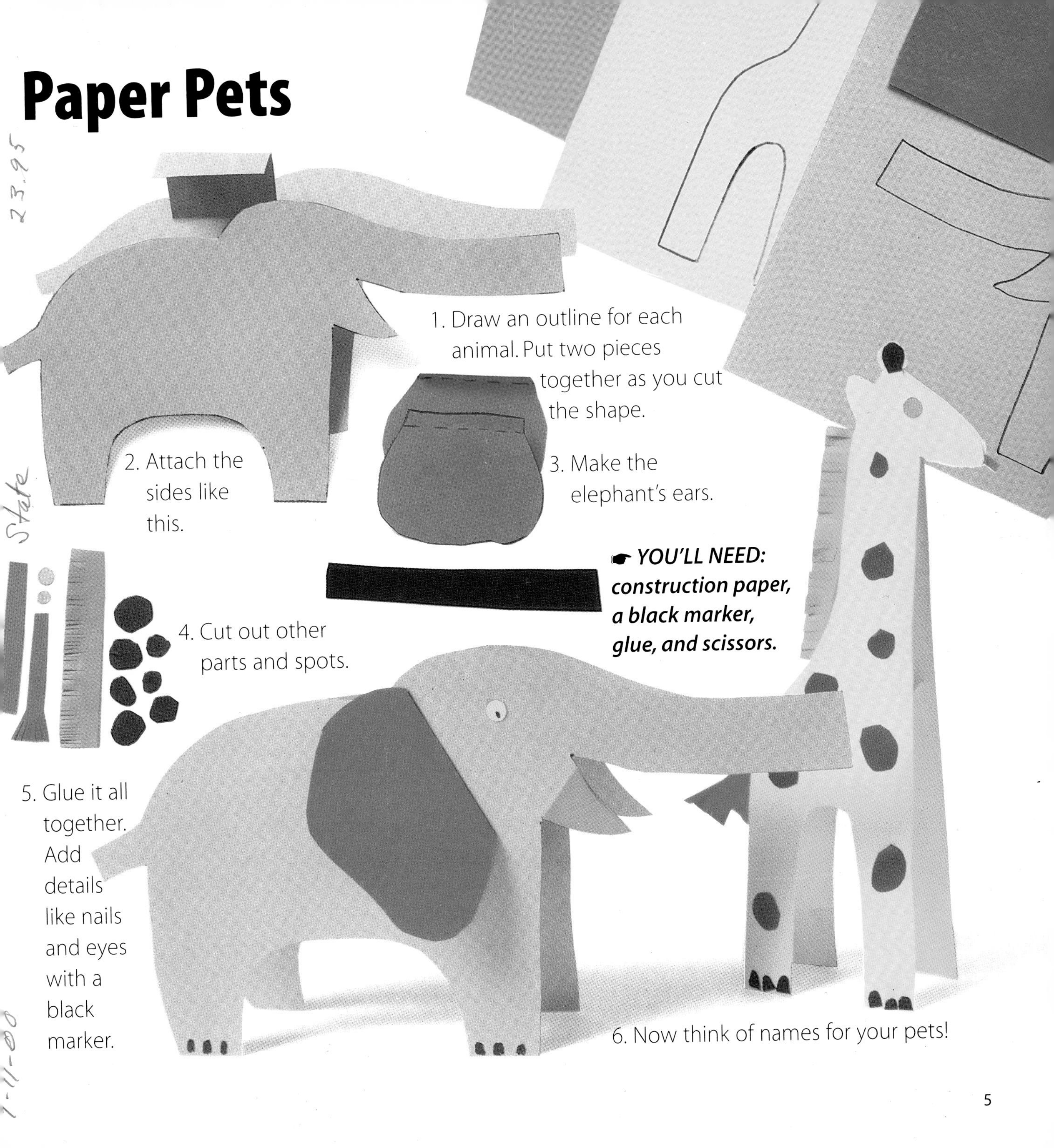

Paper Pets

1. Draw an outline for each animal. Put two pieces together as you cut the shape.

2. Attach the sides like this.

3. Make the elephant's ears.

☛ ***YOU'LL NEED: construction paper, a black marker, glue, and scissors.***

4. Cut out other parts and spots.

5. Glue it all together. Add details like nails and eyes with a black marker.

6. Now think of names for your pets!

A Vase of Fanciful Flowers

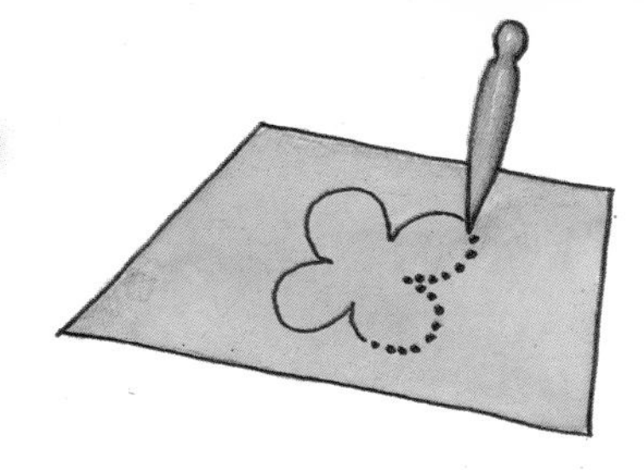

☛ ***YOU'LL NEED: various colors of construction paper, scissors, glue, push pin or pointed object, long plastic or paper straws (optional).***

1. On construction paper of different colors, draw a vase, leaves, flowers, and a vase decoration.

2. Punch out flower shapes to use as a guide when following your drawings. Ask an adult to help you.

3. Make stems out of construction paper or use straws. Glue leaves on them.

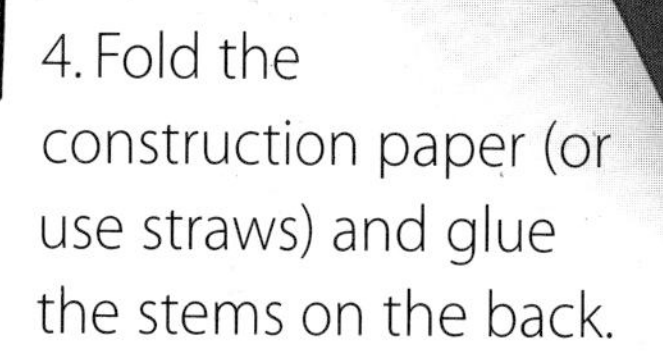

4. Fold the construction paper (or use straws) and glue the stems on the back.

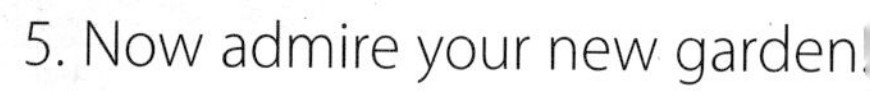

5. Now admire your new garden!

A Magazine Mosaic

☛ ***YOU'LL NEED:* a bunch of strips of magazine pages, construction paper, and glue. Cut the strips of magazine pages into small squares.**

1. Glue the squares to a sheet of construction paper in a design of your choice.
2. We chose to do a sun, but you can do anything: a spiral, flowers, even a self-portrait!

Torn Paper Projects

1. You can make many things with leftover colored papers.

☛ ***YOU'LL NEED: a large piece of construction paper for your picture's background, glue, and your torn or leftover paper.***

2. Tear the papers into different-sized pieces. Then crumple some into balls or roll them into long, thin pieces.

3. Glue the pieces onto your background. You can start with a plan or just start gluing and see what it turns into!

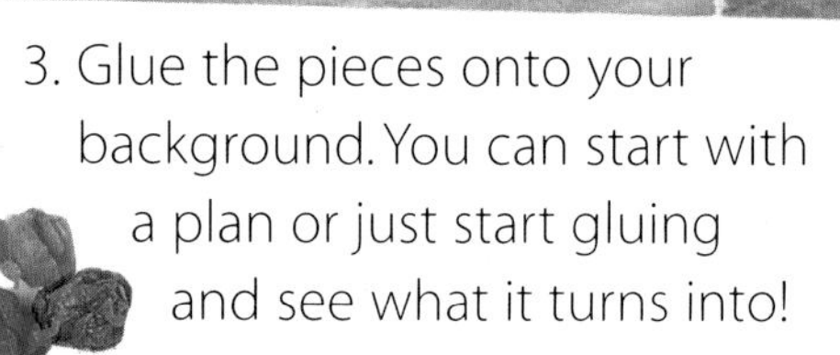

Use your imagination: *The possibilities with leftover materials are endless. Think about portraits, fantasy scenes, cars, planes, animals, even simple shapes and colors!*

Beautiful Bouquet

1. Cut flower petals in this shape. Make three for each flower. Cut leaf shapes out as well. Cut small dark circles for your flower middles.

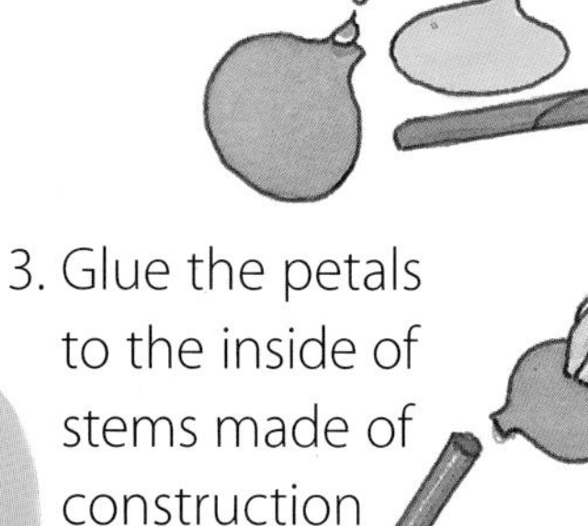

2. Put glue on each petal.

3. Glue the petals to the inside of stems made of construction paper or straws.

4. Here's how you assemble the flower pot.

☛ YOU'LL NEED: colored construction paper, glue, adhesive tape, scissors, and paper or plastic straws for stems (optional).

5. Glue leaves and the dark middles for each flower.

6. The pieces of construction paper that hold the flower stems are made by folding down the inside and gluing it to an outside ring. You'll need two holders for each bouquet. Cut three random holes in each finished holder. Then insert stems.

7. Now you have a beautiful bouquet to give to someone you love!

Use your imagination: *When you get really good, you can do other varieties of flowers. Try snipping and folding the edges of some petals for another look!*

Classic Cut-Outs

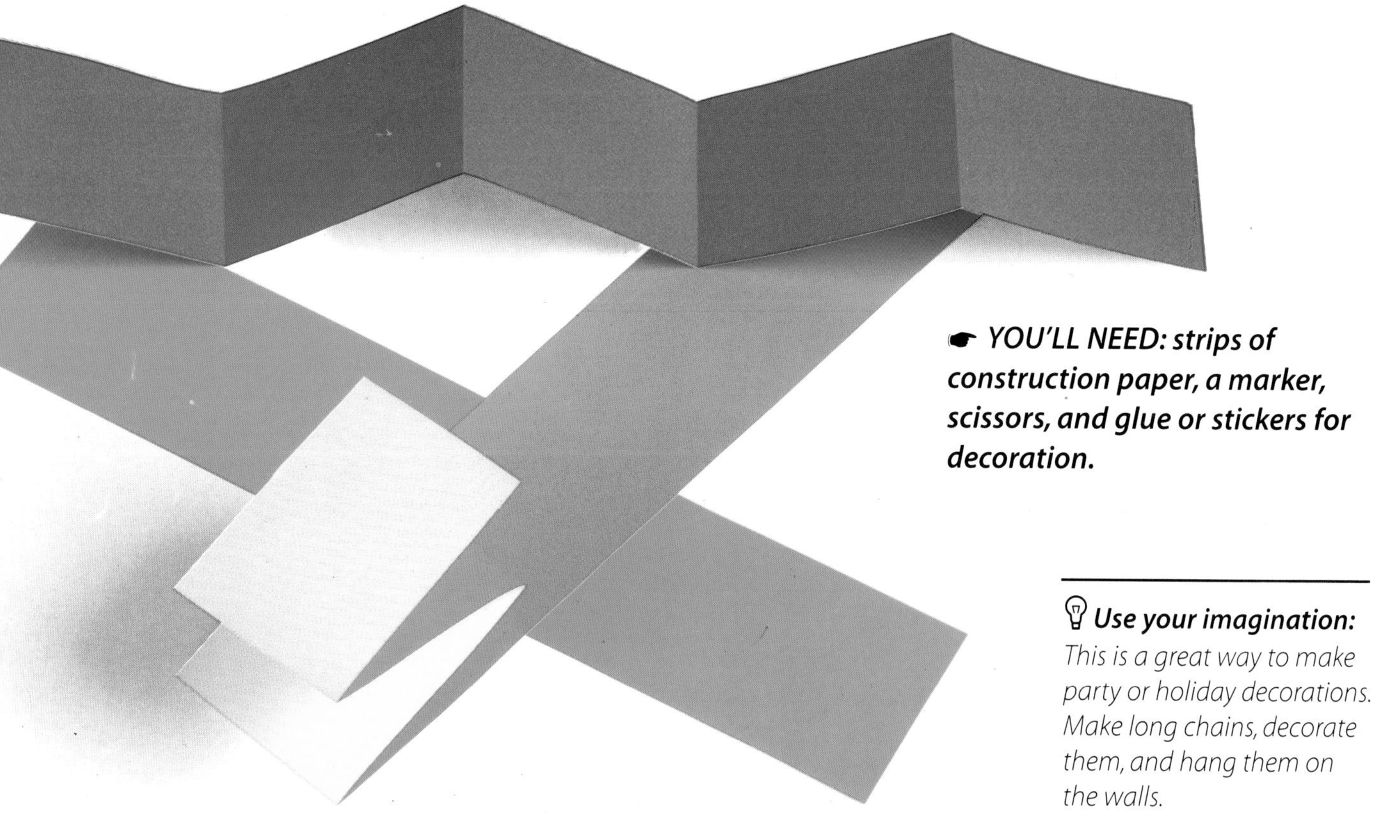

☛ ***YOU'LL NEED:** strips of construction paper, a marker, scissors, and glue or stickers for decoration.*

Use your imagination: *This is a great way to make party or holiday decorations. Make long chains, decorate them, and hang them on the walls.*

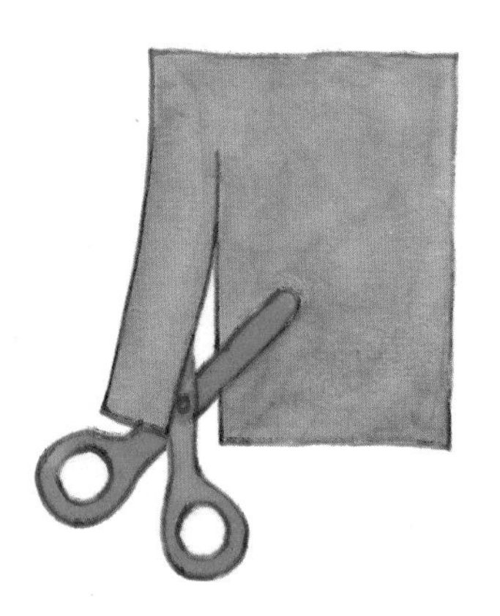

1. Cut strips of paper and fold them like an accordion.

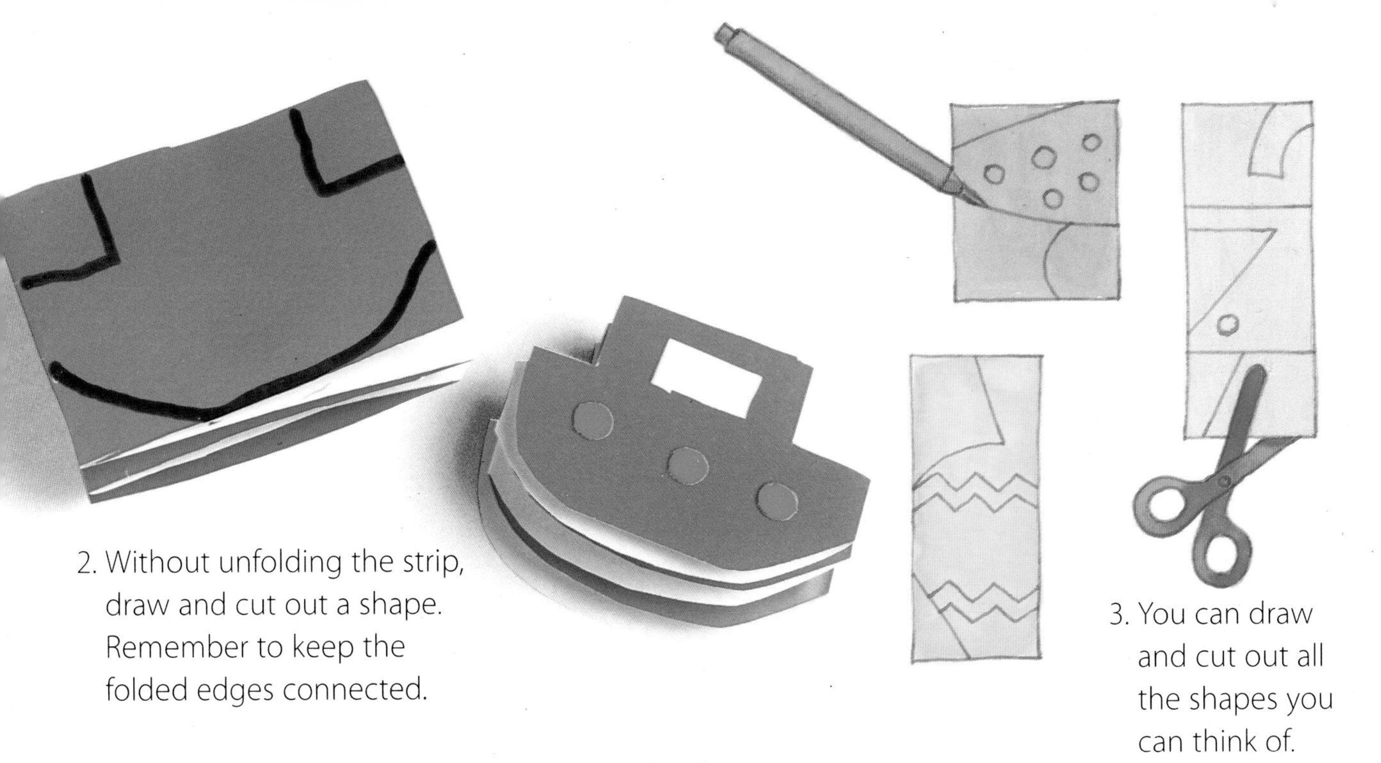

2. Without unfolding the strip, draw and cut out a shape. Remember to keep the folded edges connected.

3. You can draw and cut out all the shapes you can think of.

4. Open the strips and decorate your creations with stickers or by gluing small pieces of colored paper.

A Circle of Friends

☛ ***YOU'LL NEED: construction paper in different colors, a marker, glue, and scissors.***

1. Cut out hair and cut out and draw faces.

2. Fold construction paper like this and draw half a figure on one side.

3. Cut the folded paper. Unfold it and you'll have a complete figure.

4. To make clothes, place construction paper over the figure and cut out a dress or pants.

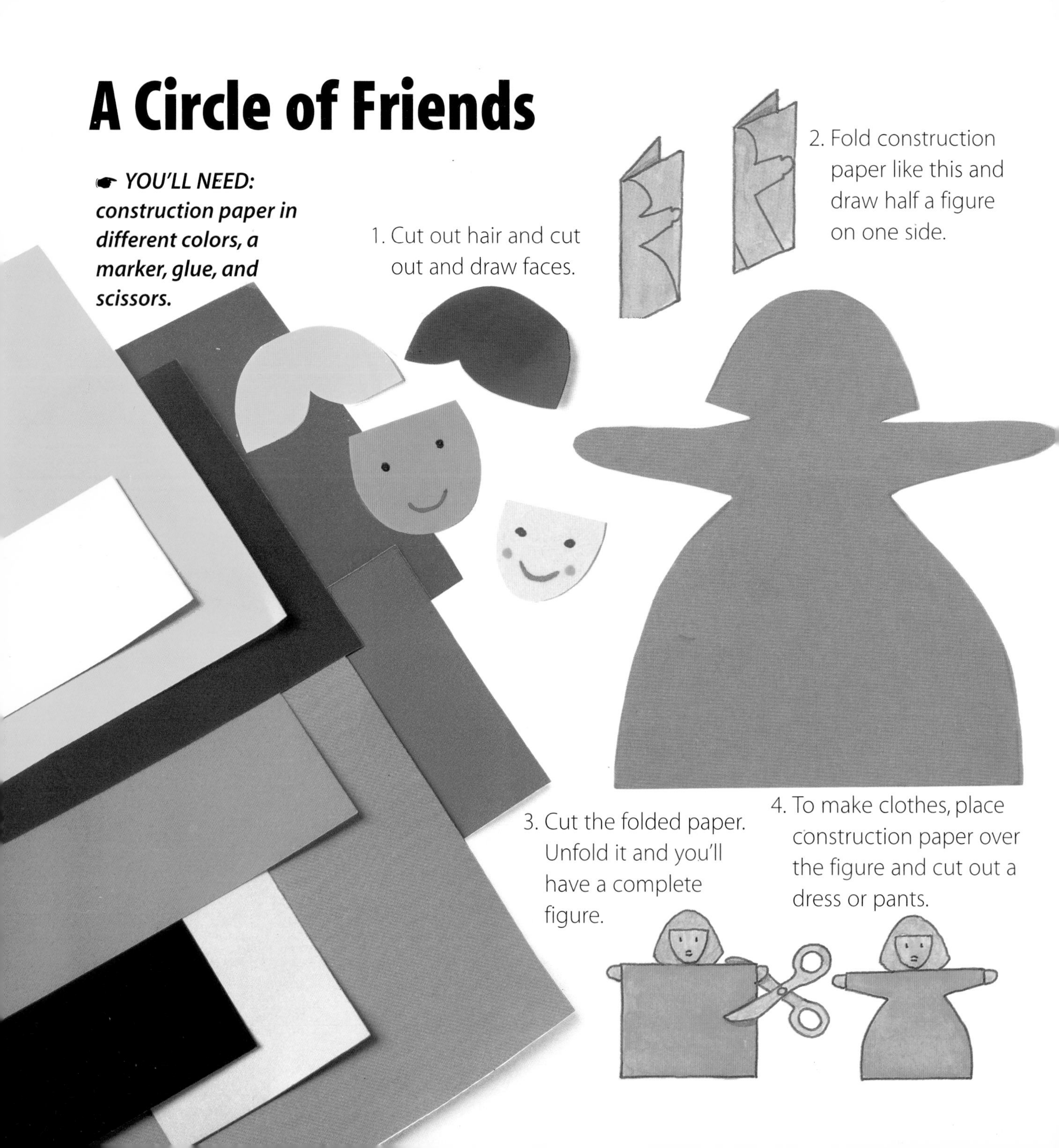

5. Glue your friends to each other by the hands in a long row.
6. Glue on their faces, dresses, and pants. Then add their hair. Draw details with a black marker.
7. When your friends are done, tape the two ends of your row together to form a circle.

Use your imagination:

Can you make a circle of friends from different countries? Find pictures of different flags and draw them on the clothes of each friend!

A Magical Fold-Down Forest

☛ ***YOU'LL NEED:** sheets of construction paper, glue, a marker, scissors, and stickers (optional).*

1. Fold a sheet of construction paper and cut strips of different lengths and widths.

2. Separate and lift the strips and then unfold the sheet.

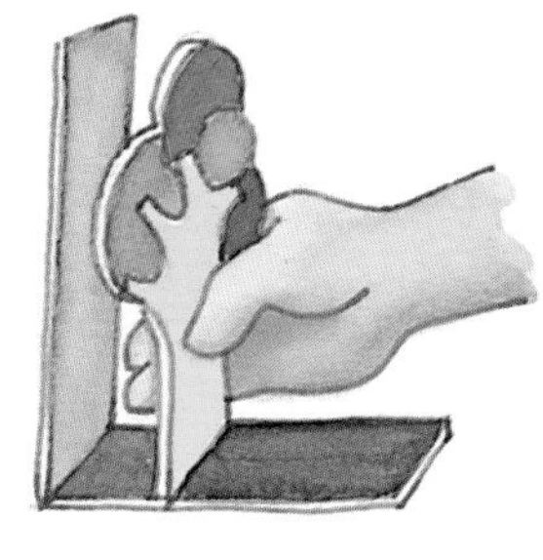

3. Cut out trees, stars, animals, a river, bushes, flowers, or whatever you'd like in your scene. Glue your pieces to the strips or to the background. Add stickers for decoration, if you like.

4. When you flatten the sheet, the drawings will also go down.

Use your imagination: *You can create any scene this way. How about making some fold-down circus performers or some fold-down flowers? You could even do a fold-down skyline with tall buildings and a city!*

A Chicken Change Box

☛ ***YOU'LL NEED: colored construction paper, an empty matchbox, glue, and scissors.***

1. Cut a piece of construction paper the width of the matchbox and cover it by gluing.

2. Draw the head of a rooster on folded construction paper and cut it out. Also cut out the tail, beak, and eyes.

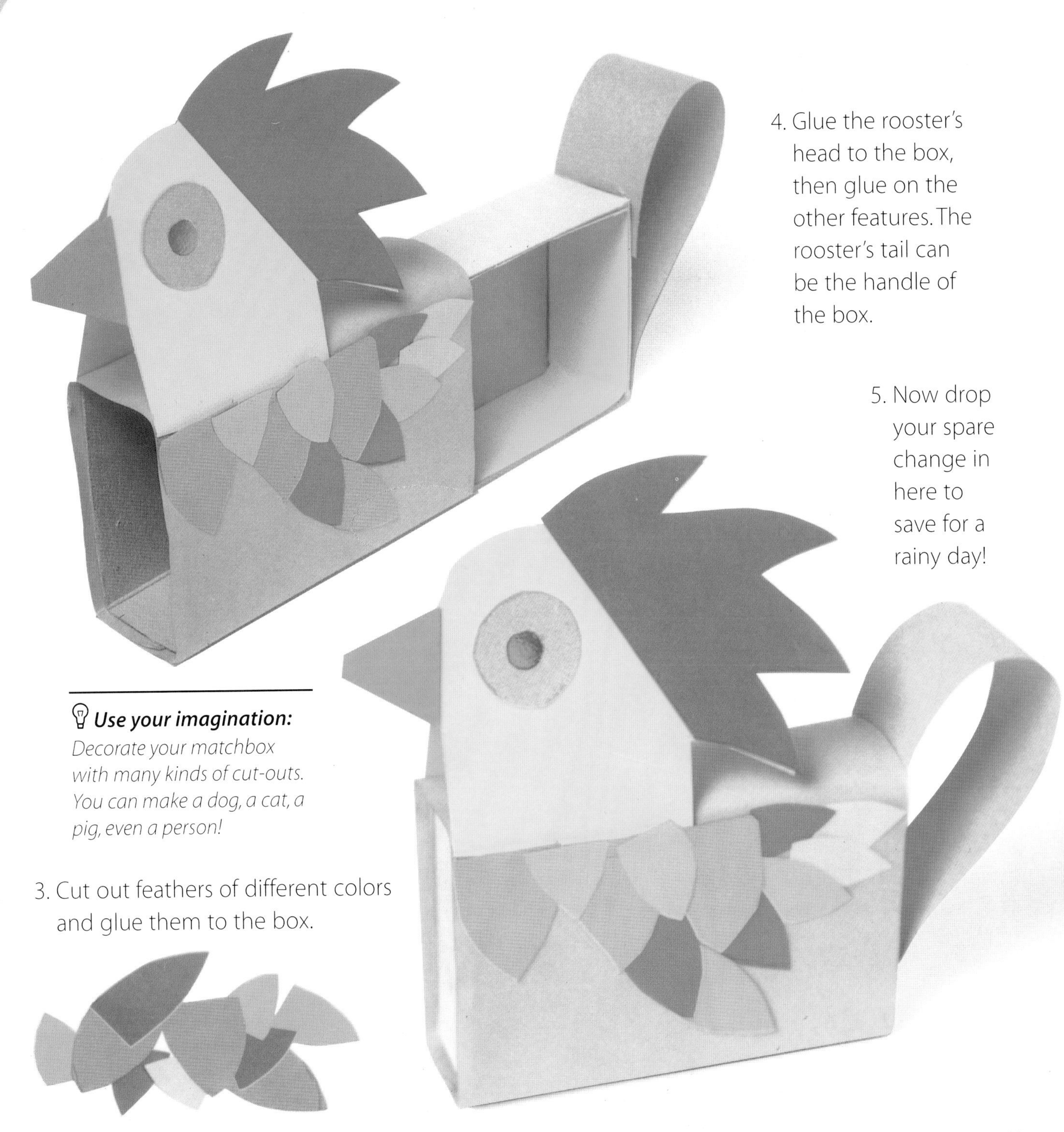

4. Glue the rooster's head to the box, then glue on the other features. The rooster's tail can be the handle of the box.

5. Now drop your spare change in here to save for a rainy day!

Use your imagination:
Decorate your matchbox with many kinds of cut-outs. You can make a dog, a cat, a pig, even a person!

3. Cut out feathers of different colors and glue them to the box.

A Wonderful Wildlife Mobile

☛ ***YOU'LL NEED: various colors of construction paper, glue, string, and scissors.***

1. On construction paper of different colors, draw the outlines of all the fish and the birds without their wings.

2. Fold the paper at the beak or mouth and cut out the shapes.

3. Make wings by folding construction paper like an accordion.

4. Glue together the two sides of each shape. Leave the backs of the birds open for the tail.

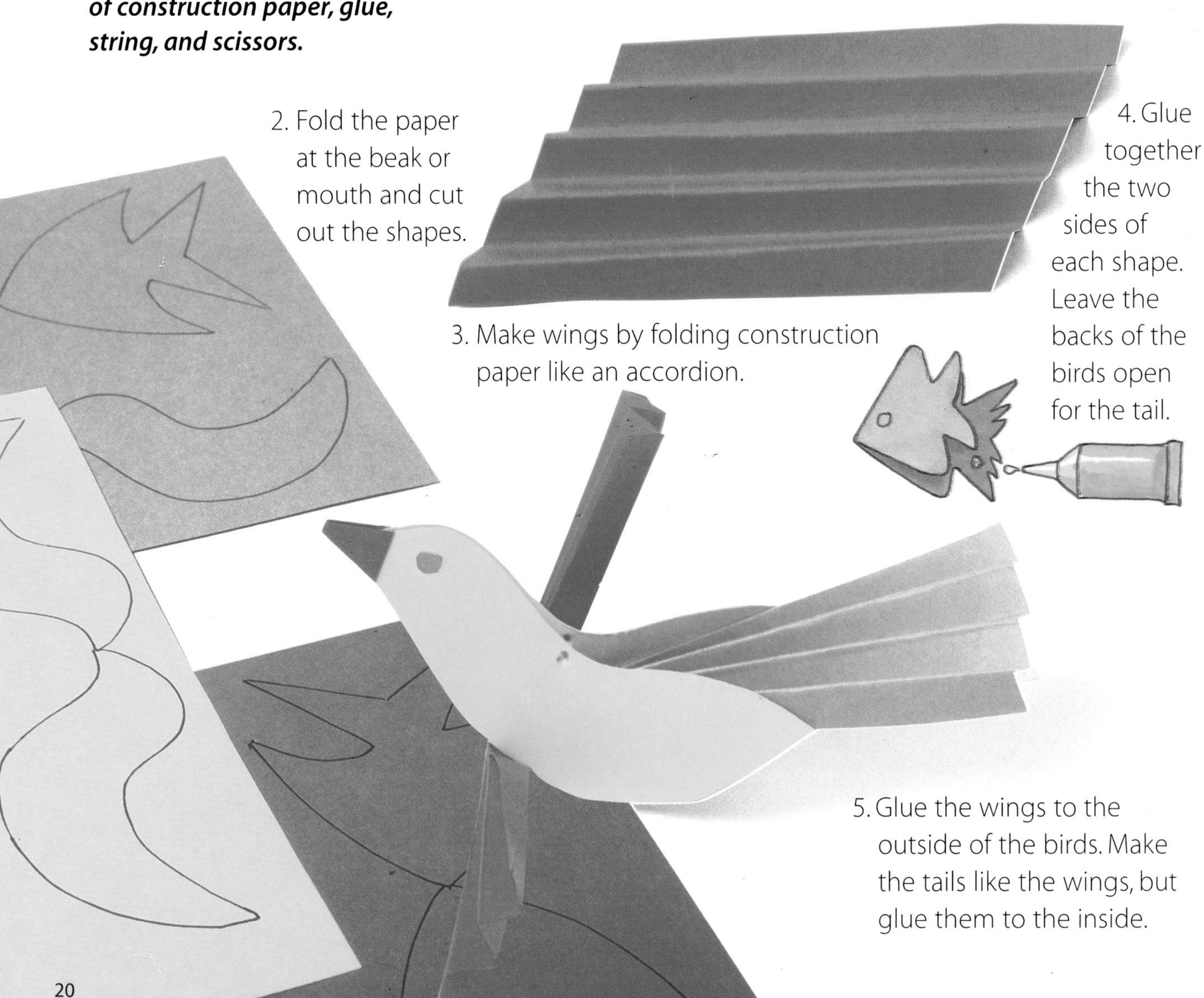

5. Glue the wings to the outside of the birds. Make the tails like the wings, but glue them to the inside.

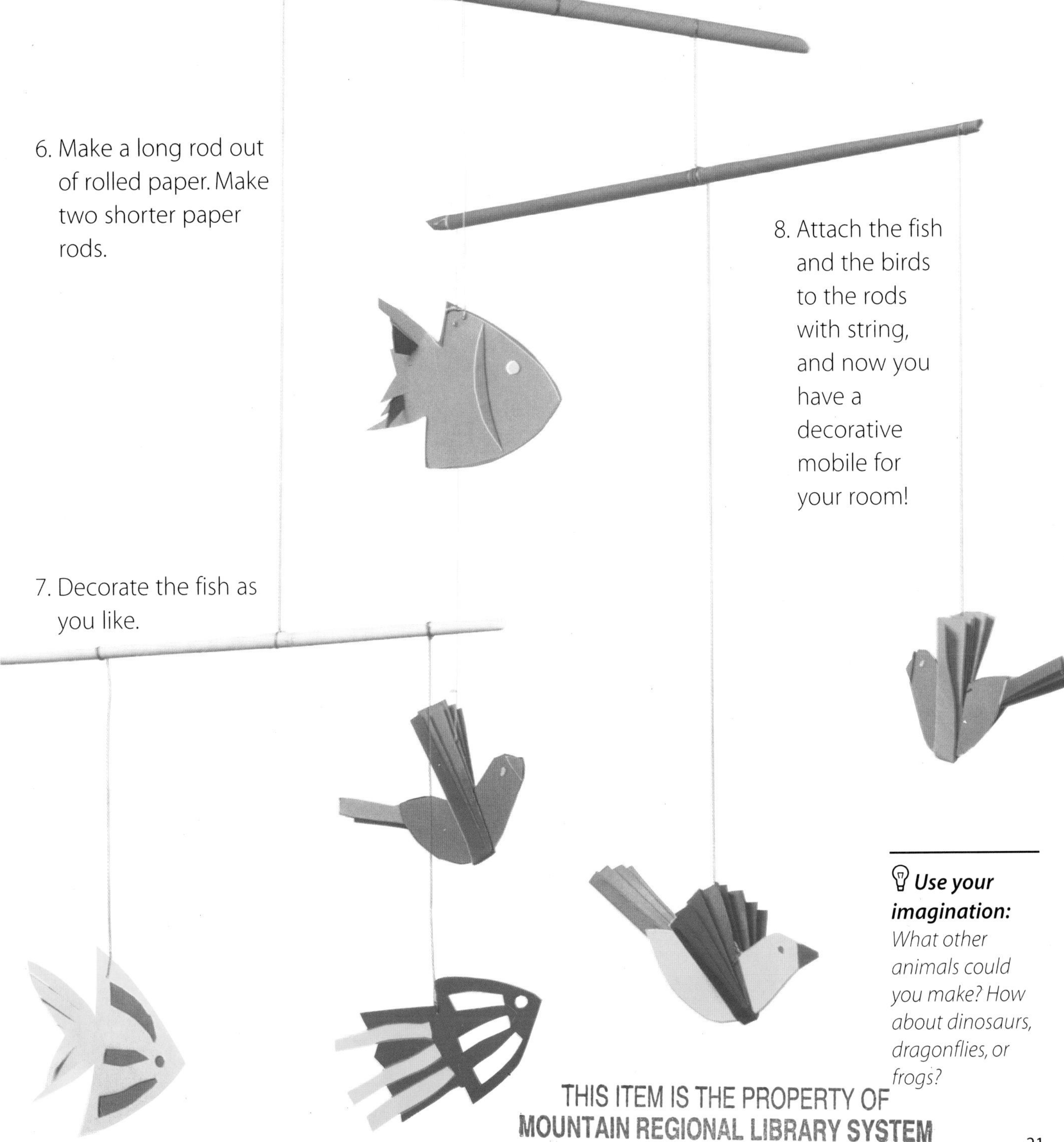

6. Make a long rod out of rolled paper. Make two shorter paper rods.

7. Decorate the fish as you like.

8. Attach the fish and the birds to the rods with string, and now you have a decorative mobile for your room!

Use your imagination: *What other animals could you make? How about dinosaurs, dragonflies, or frogs?*

Jazzy Jewelry

☛ ***YOU'LL NEED: sheets of construction paper, a hole punch, colored markers, adhesive tape, glue, elastic cord, and scissors.***

1. To make dot bracelets, hole punch or have an adult help cut out different colored paper, and save the dots. Glue them to the strips. Now join the ends of two strips of construction paper.

2. To make crinkle-style bracelets, place one long strip of construction paper over another like this.

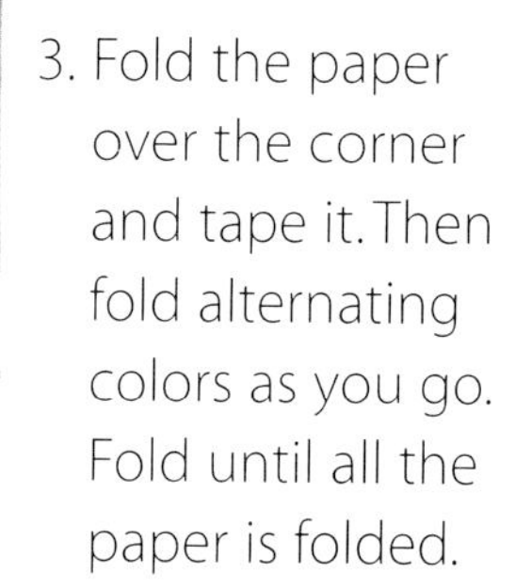

3. Fold the paper over the corner and tape it. Then fold alternating colors as you go. Fold until all the paper is folded.

4. Pull on both ends at once to elongate the band. Then tape the two ends together.

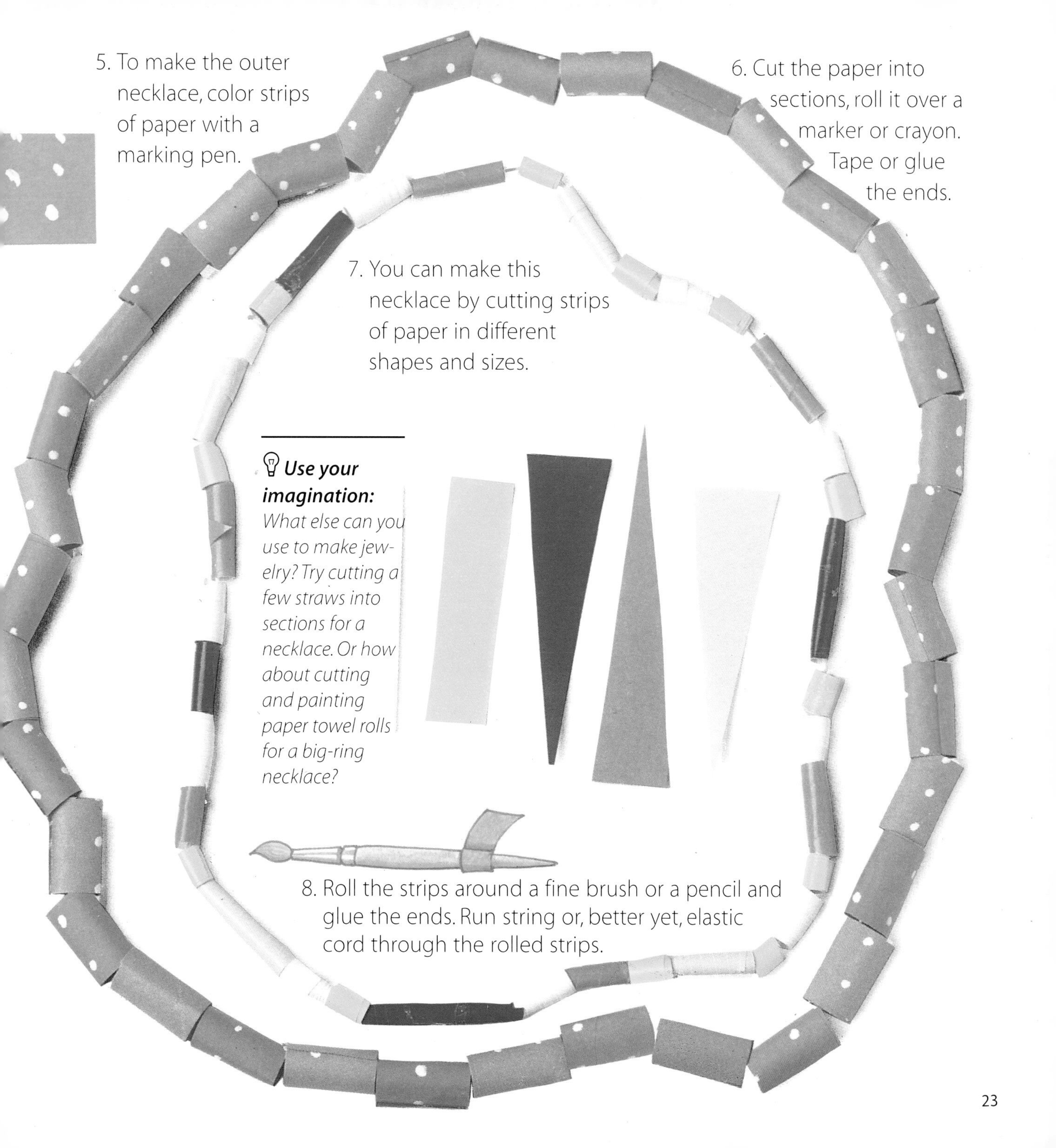

5. To make the outer necklace, color strips of paper with a marking pen.

6. Cut the paper into sections, roll it over a marker or crayon. Tape or glue the ends.

7. You can make this necklace by cutting strips of paper in different shapes and sizes.

Use your imagination:
What else can you use to make jewelry? Try cutting a few straws into sections for a necklace. Or how about cutting and painting paper towel rolls for a big-ring necklace?

8. Roll the strips around a fine brush or a pencil and glue the ends. Run string or, better yet, elastic cord through the rolled strips.

A Playtime Pinwheel

☛ ***YOU'LL NEED: two sheets of different-colored construction paper, a paper clip, a round piece of construction paper, a wooden or heavy cardboard rod, a cork, and glue.***

1. Place the colored paper sheets one on top of the other.

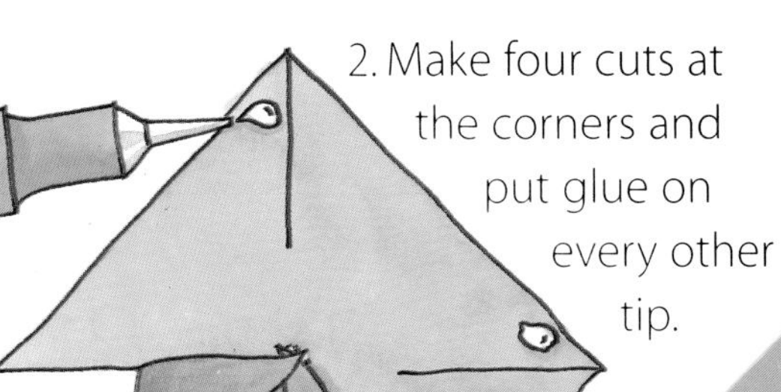

2. Make four cuts at the corners and put glue on every other tip.

3. Open up the paper clip like this. (Ask an adult for help if you need to.)

4. Bend and glue the same-color tips together like this.

5. Assemble the clip, the round piece of construction paper, the pinwheel, the rod, and the cork as shown.

6. Now, give it a blow and make it spin!

Use your imagination:
You can make "special effects" as your pinwheel turns by painting or drawing circles on the spokes. You could even decorate it with glow-in-the-dark stickers!

A Halloween or Costume Ball Mask

☛ ***YOU'LL NEED:***
construction paper in different colors, tissue paper, a ribbon, glue, and scissors.

1. Draw and cut out the mask in the shape shown. You can also change the shape to make pointy cheeks or a differently shaped head.

2. Draw and cut out the feathers as shown. Cut out two circles of tissue paper for cheeks. Make a diamond-shaped piece for a beak or nose.

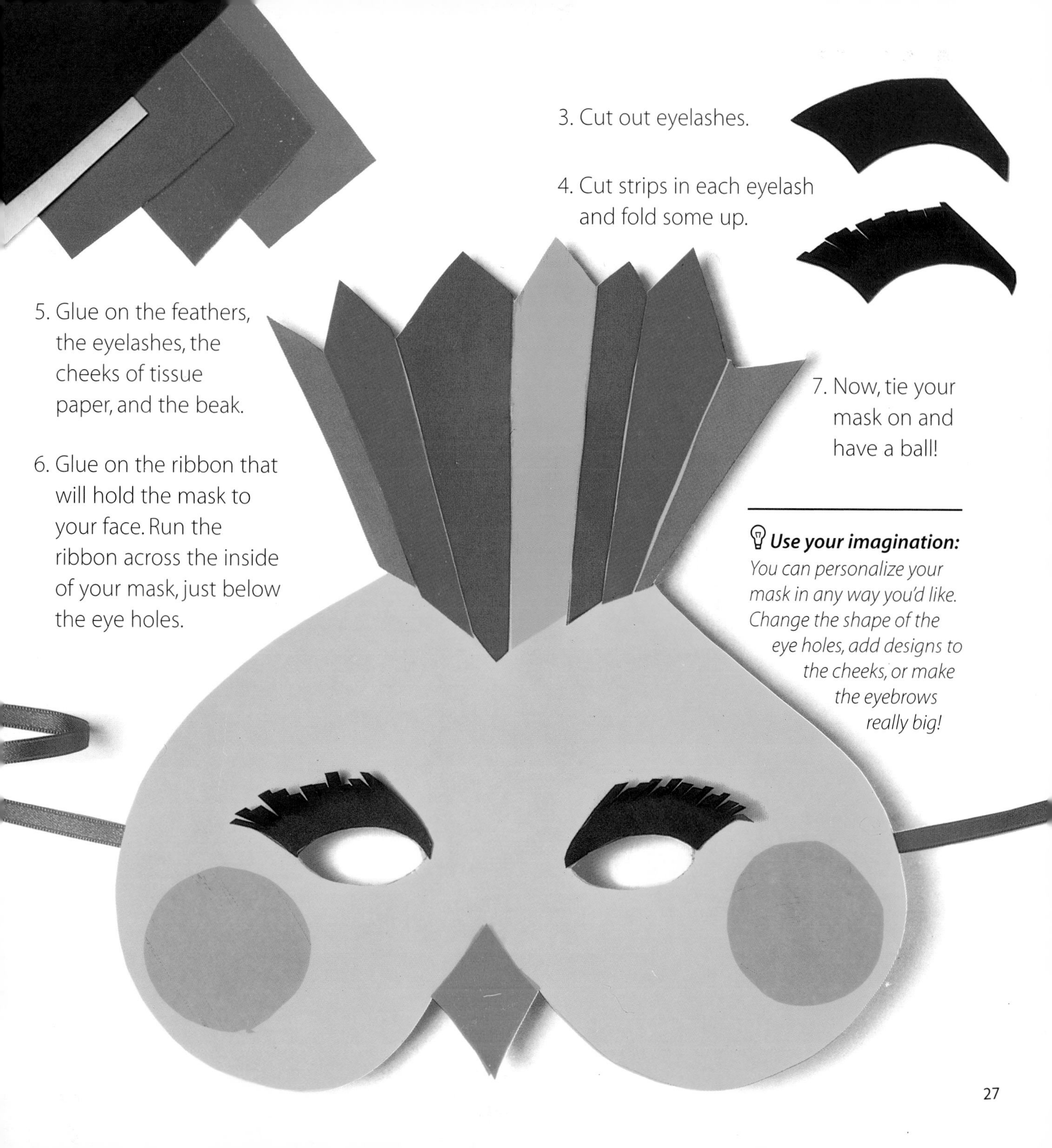

3. Cut out eyelashes.

4. Cut strips in each eyelash and fold some up.

5. Glue on the feathers, the eyelashes, the cheeks of tissue paper, and the beak.

6. Glue on the ribbon that will hold the mask to your face. Run the ribbon across the inside of your mask, just below the eye holes.

7. Now, tie your mask on and have a ball!

Use your imagination:
You can personalize your mask in any way you'd like. Change the shape of the eye holes, add designs to the cheeks, or make the eyebrows really big!

Funtime Furniture

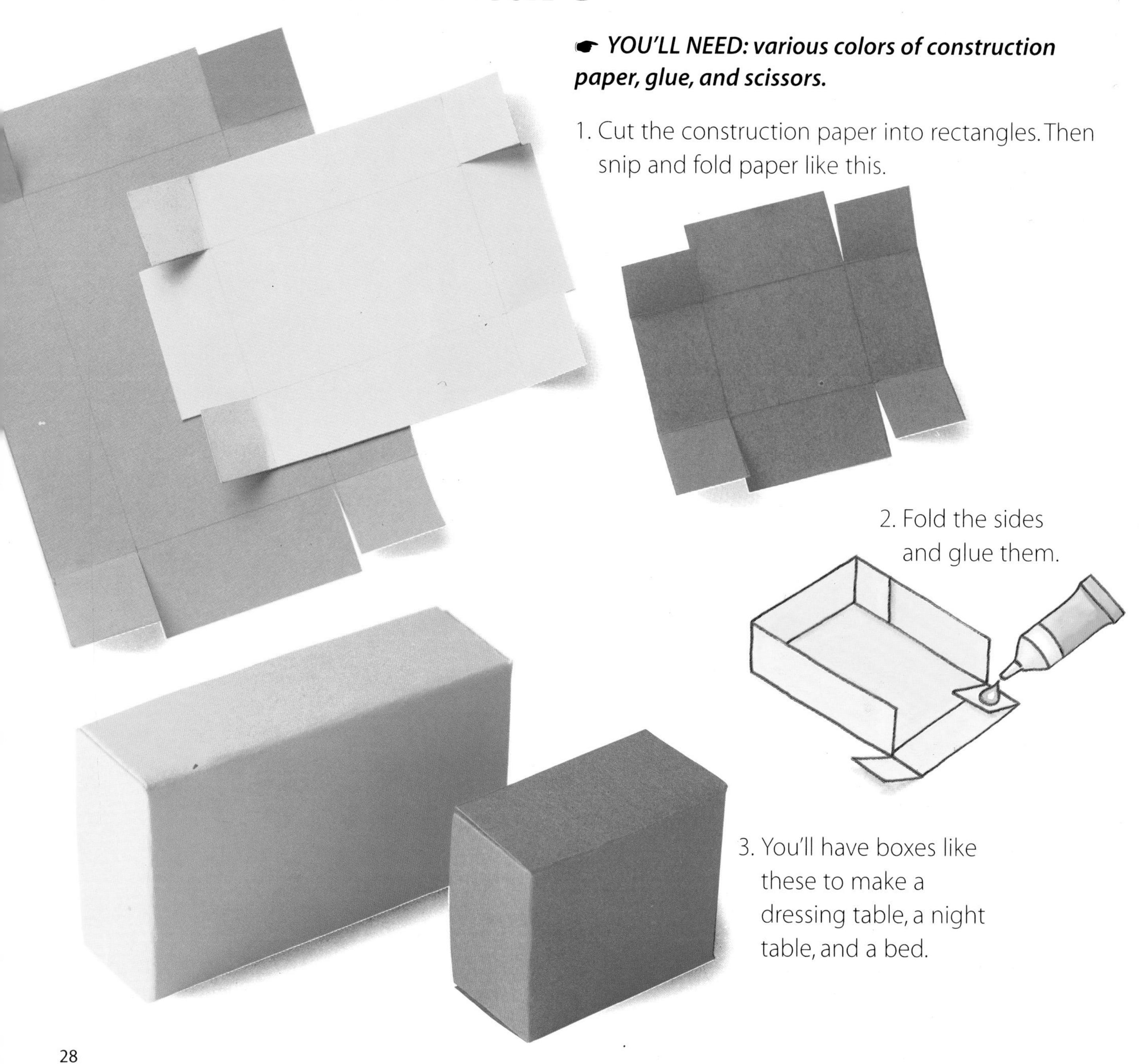

☛ ***YOU'LL NEED: various colors of construction paper, glue, and scissors.***

1. Cut the construction paper into rectangles. Then snip and fold paper like this.

2. Fold the sides and glue them.

3. You'll have boxes like these to make a dressing table, a night table, and a bed.

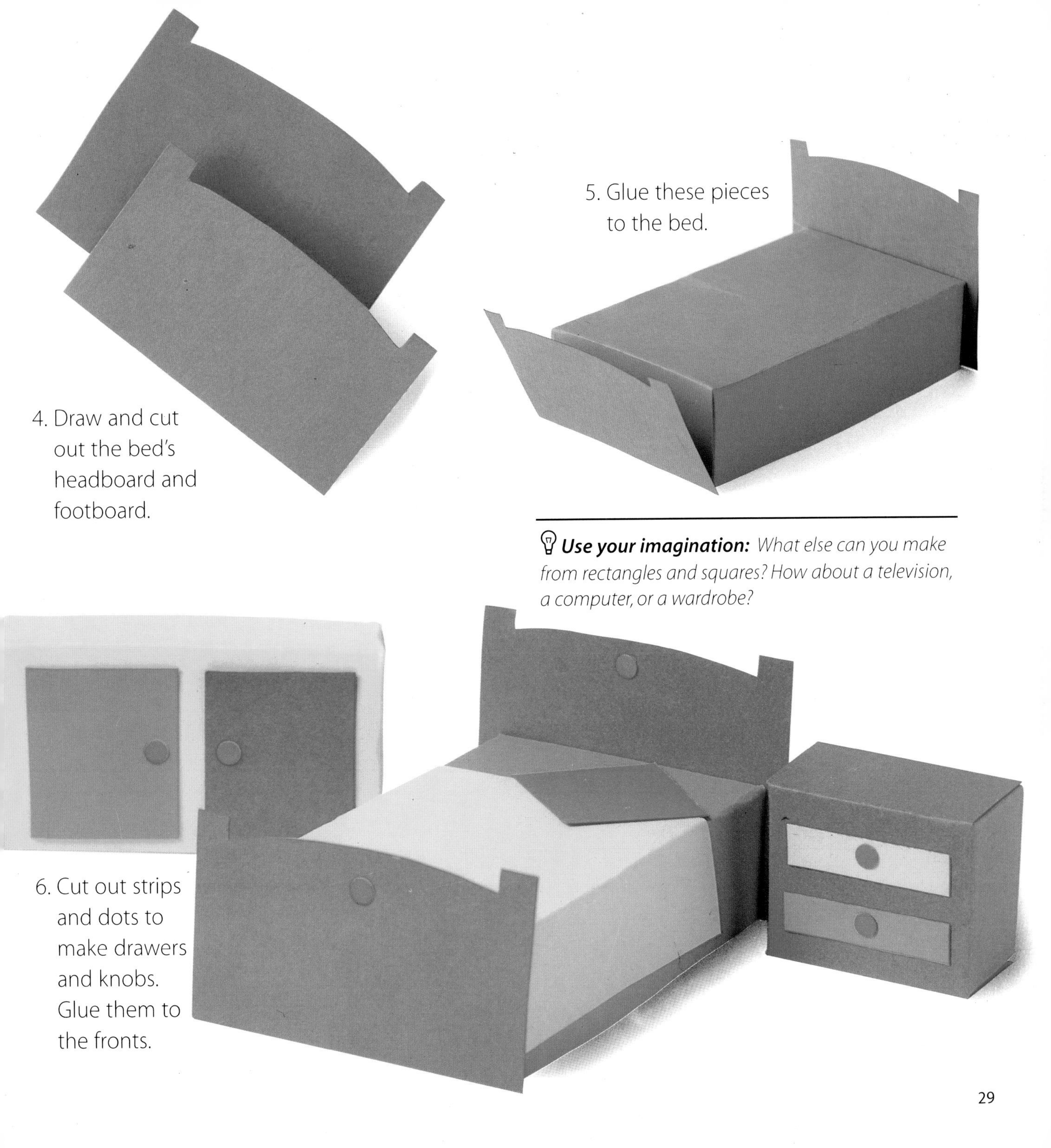

4. Draw and cut out the bed's headboard and footboard.

5. Glue these pieces to the bed.

💡 ***Use your imagination:*** *What else can you make from rectangles and squares? How about a television, a computer, or a wardrobe?*

6. Cut out strips and dots to make drawers and knobs. Glue them to the fronts.

WHERE TO GET SUPPLIES

Art & Woodcrafters Supply, Inc.
www.artwoodcrafter.com
Order a catalog or browse online for many different craft supplies.

Craft Supplies
www.craftsfaironline.com/Supplies.html
This online craft store features many different sites, each featuring products for specific hobbies.

Darice, Inc.
21160 Drake Road
Strongsville, OH 44136-6699
www.darice.com
Order a catalog or browse online for many different craft supplies.

Making Friends
www.makingfriends.com
Offers many kits and products for children's crafts.

National Artcraft
7996 Darrow Road
Twinsburg, OH 44087
www.nationalartcraft.com
This craft store features many products available through its catalog or online.

FOR MORE INFORMATION

Books

Chapman, Gillian. *Autumn* (Seasonal Crafts). Chatham, NJ: Raintree/Steck Vaughn, 1997.

Chapman, Gillian. Pam Robson (Contributor). *Art From Fabric: With Projects Using Rags, Old Clothes, and Remnants.* New York, NY: Thomson Learning, 1995.

Connor, Nikki. Sarah Jean Neaves (Illustrator). *Cardboard Boxes* (Creating Crafts From). Providence, RI: Copper Beech Books, 1996.

Gordon, Lynn. *52 Great Art Projects For Kids.* San Francisco, CA: Chronicle Books, 1996.

King, Penny. Clare Roundhill (Contributor). *Animals* (Artists' Workshop). New York, NY: Crabtree Publishing, 1996.

Ross, Kathy. Sharon Lane Holm (Illustrator). *The Best Holiday Crafts Ever*. Brookfield, CT: Millbrook Publishing, 1996.

Smith, Alistair. *Big Book of Papercraft*. Newton, MA: Educational Development Center, 1996.

Videos

Blue's Clues Arts & Crafts. Nickelodeon. (1998).

Web Sites

Crafts For Kids
www.craftsforkids.miningco.com/mbody.htm
Many different arts and crafts activities are explained in detail.

Family Crafts
www.family.go.com
Search for crafts by age group. Projects include instructions, supply list, and helpful tips.

KinderCrafts
www.EnchantedLearning.com/Crafts
Step-by-step instructions explain how to make
animal, dinosaur, box, and paper crafts, plus much more.

Making Friends
www.makingfriends.com
Contains hundreds of craft ideas with detailed instructions for children ages 2 to 12, including paper dolls, summer crafts, yucky stuff, and holiday crafts.

INDEX